Making an Ocean Ecosystem

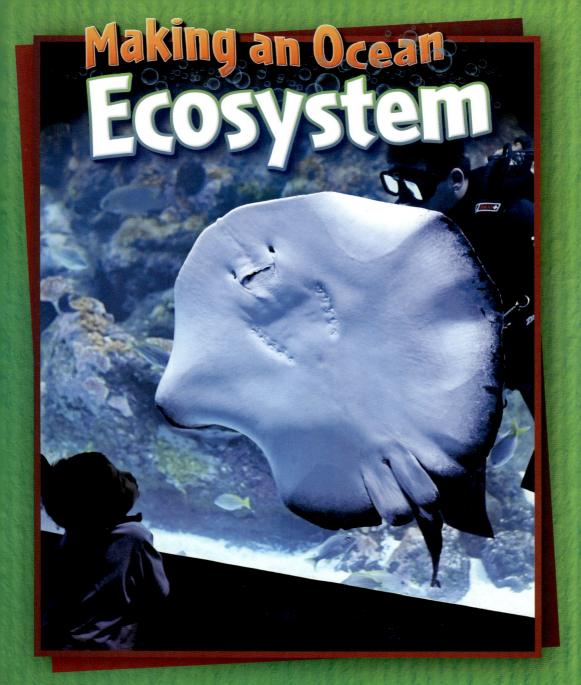

Lisa Holewa

© 2019 Smithsonian Institution. The name "Smithsonian" and the Smithsonian logo are registered trademarks owned by the Smithsonian Institution.

Contributing Author

Allison Duarte

Consultants

Jessica Lunt, Ph.D.
Marine Biologist
Smithsonian Marine Station

Stephanie Anastasopoulos, M.Ed.
TOSA, STREAM Integration
Solana Beach School District

Publishing Credits

Rachelle Cracchiolo, M.S.Ed., *Publisher*
Conni Medina, M.A.Ed., *Managing Editor*
Diana Kenney, M.A.Ed., NBCT, *Content Director*
Véronique Bos, *Creative Director*
Robin Erickson, *Art Director*
Michelle Jovin, M.A., *Associate Editor*
Mindy Duits, *Senior Graphic Designer*
Smithsonian Science Education Center

Image Credits: front cover, p.1 David Clode/Unsplash; p.7 (top) imagesandstories/picture alliance/blickwinkel/Newscom; p.9 (top) David Doubilet/National Geographic/Getty Images; p.10 Dennis Kunkel Microscopy/Science Source; p.11 (top and bottom left), 19 (bottom left) Dennis Kunkel Microscopy/Science Source; p.13 (bottom) Ann Ronan Picture Library Heritage Images/Newscom; pp.16–17 Glenn Beanlan/Getty Images; p.18 LeonP/Shutterstock; p.20 Reinhard Dirscherl/Science Source; p.22 (top) Paulo Oliveira/Alamy; p.23 (map) Carol and Mike Werner/Science Source; p.24 (bottom left) John De Mello/Alamy; p.25 (left) Citizen of the Planet/Alamy; p.27 (top) Peter Bennett/Science Source; back cover (top left) Gerd Guenther/Science Source; back cover (right) © Smithsonian; all other images from iStock and/or Shutterstock.

Library of Congress Cataloging-in-Publication Data

Names: Holewa, Lisa, author.
Title: Making an ocean ecosystem / Lisa Holewa.
Description: Huntington Beach, CA : Teacher Created Materials, Inc., [2019] | Audience: Grade 4 to 6. | Includes index. |
Identifiers: LCCN 2018022267 (print) | LCCN 2018024511 (ebook) | ISBN 9781493869602 (E-book) | ISBN 9781493867202 (paperback)
Subjects: LCSH: Marine microbial ecology--Juvenile literature.
Classification: LCC QR106 (ebook) | LCC QR106 .H65 2019 (print) | DDC 579/.177--dc23
LC record available at https://lccn.loc.gov/2018022267

Smithsonian

© 2019 Smithsonian Institution. The name "Smithsonian" and the Smithsonian logo are registered trademarks owned by the Smithsonian Institution.

Teacher Created Materials

5301 Oceanus Drive
Huntington Beach, CA 92649-1030
www.tcmpub.com

ISBN 978-1-4938-6720-2
© 2019 Teacher Created Materials, Inc.
Printed in China
Nordica.102018.CA21801129

Table of Contents

Underwater Worlds 4

Studying the Marine Environment 6

Marine Microbes 10

Putting It All Together 14

Creatures Big and Small 26

STEAM Challenge 28

Glossary 30

Index 31

Career Advice 32

Underwater Worlds

There are many worlds to explore under water. They can be in shallow, sandy lakes. Or they can be deep within the ocean. Entire **ecosystems** exist when you venture off land.

Marine ecosystems exist along coral reefs. They exist within **mangrove** forests. They are along limestone ledges. They're within seagrasses close to the coastline.

Scuba divers explore these worlds. Sometimes, they are shallow enough for snorkelers to see. Other times, only scientists in submarines can reach them. Or they might be displayed for everyone to see at museums or zoos.

A pygmy seahorse blends in with red coral.

Aquariums have tanks that model marine ecosystems. They re-create underwater worlds. People often enjoy watching the biggest creatures in these tanks. They notice the most unique or most colorful creatures. Jellies and sea stars are fun to watch. It's hard not to wonder about seahorses and sea urchins. Blue crabs and spiny lobsters draw attention.

But, what about creatures too tiny to see? Do bacteria exist in the sea? Do microbes affect ocean life? Can the smallest creatures in underwater worlds also be the mightiest?

spiny lobster

Bacteria come in many shapes, such as spheres, rods, and spirals.

5

Studying the Marine Environment

Aquarium tanks allow people to see marine environments more closely. They help people understand more about underwater worlds. Hopefully, they also inspire people to take care of oceans and lakes—and the creatures that live in them.

Tanks also help scientists. Sometimes, they study model ecosystems to learn more about how certain changes affect marine life. Many big aquariums hire researchers. Their job is to learn more about life under water. Researchers work with aquarists. Aquarists take care of creatures at aquariums.

Sea lions swim in an aquarium filled with giant kelp.

A Display for All

Aquarists want fish in a tank to act as they do in nature. Having the right plants and rock formations can make sea creatures feel right at home. But aquarists must balance this with the need for the public to easily see the animals. If there are too many places for fish to hide, visitors won't see them and won't want to come back.

Untangling the Food Web

Aquarium researchers study marine food webs. A food web is a bit like a food chain. But it shows many different ways marine plants and animals are connected.

Sea jellies, for instance, were once thought of mainly as predators. They eat the eggs of many sea creatures. They didn't seem as though they would be good food for other fish because they are mostly water. Now, we know that many sea creatures *do* eat sea jellies. Penguins and sea turtles consider them a good snack!

Researchers also know that some squid are cannibals. Their research shows that swordfish, whales, and seals eat squid too. This is just another way in which marine food webs are very complex.

A sea turtle eats a jellyfish.

Changes in the Water

Aquarium researchers also study how marine creatures find their food in the water. But pollution can change water. That makes it hard for animals to eat and stay healthy. And scientists are learning about other threats.

Scientists know that carbon dioxide (CO_2) levels have changed the **atmosphere**. But are they changing underwater worlds too? Researchers are trying to find out by measuring levels of CO_2 in samples of water. Levels are increasing. This might be bad news for some coral. They need certain conditions to grow. And CO_2 makes seawater more **acidic**. It affects the conditions that let coral grow.

Some aquarium researchers are trying to learn more about how CO_2 affects freshwater lakes. Does it make the water harmful for creatures who live there? Does it make it harder for them to find food? There is much to learn.

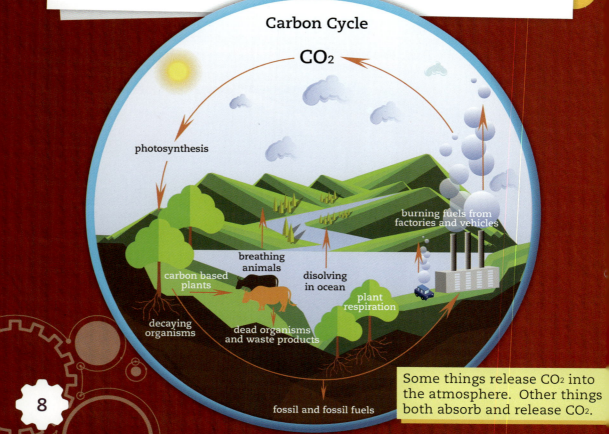

Some things release CO_2 into the atmosphere. Other things both absorb and release CO_2.

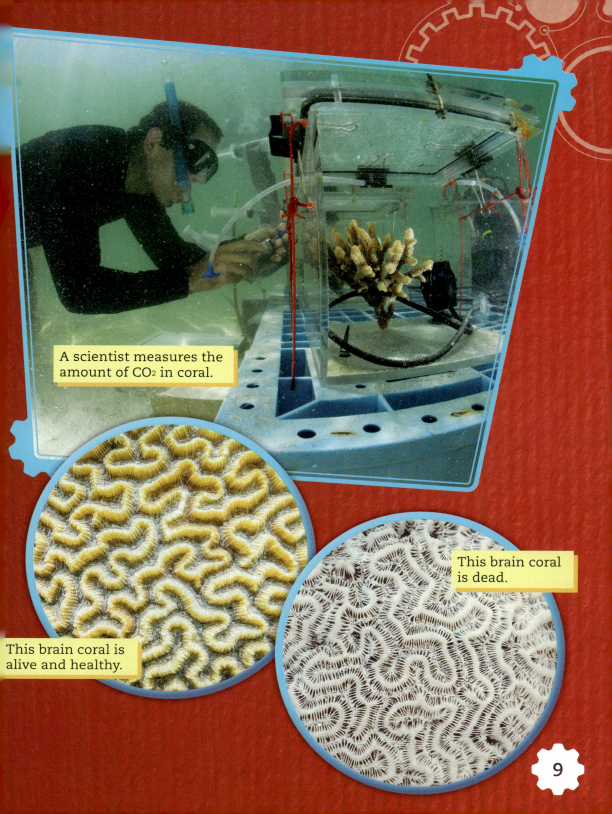

A scientist measures the amount of CO_2 in coral.

This brain coral is dead.

This brain coral is alive and healthy.

Marine Microbes

Creating a marine ecosystem on land is not easy. It requires an understanding of underwater worlds. Small changes have big effects.

Bacteria Are Everywhere

Microbes are creatures so small they cannot be seen without microscopes. But they are everywhere. In fact, microbes make up 98 percent of the **biomass** of the planet's oceans.

Many of those microbes are bacteria. Scientists have known for a long time that bacteria affects life on land. But they are now working to understand the role of bacteria in lakes and oceans. New technology is giving them tools to study bacteria's effects. This is a growing field of science. It is called marine microbial ecology.

One thing scientists know is that bacteria are key to life in the ocean. They are necessary in the nitrogen cycle. This is true on land and in water. Nitrogen makes up most of the air we breathe. But this type of nitrogen cannot be used by most organisms. In the ocean, marine bacteria help change it into a type of nitrogen that other marine life can use.

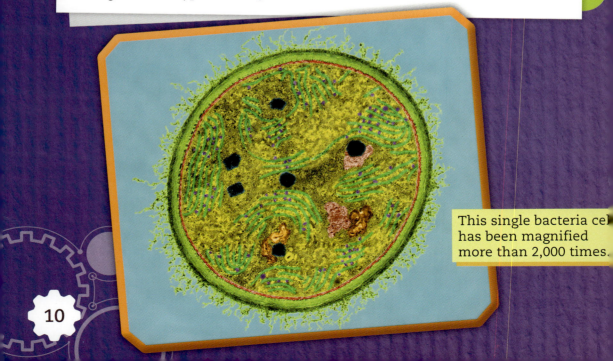

This single bacteria cell has been magnified more than 2,000 times.

One milliliter (0.2 teaspoons) of sea water can hold up to a million microbes. Eight liters (2 gallons) of seawater hold more bacteria than there are people on Earth.

Decomposition is another important part of the nitrogen cycle. Marine bacteria decompose organisms that have died. These organisms can be as big as whales. They can be as small as tiny microbes. Either way, bacteria help break down **molecules** that made the creature. This makes their nutrients available for other organisms to use.

Many different types of microbes live in the oceans. They all play different and key roles in the nitrogen cycle. They are vital to the marine CO_2 cycle too. Microbes also help in other ways. Some elements, such as iron, are hard to find in the ocean. Microbes can catch iron released by dead organisms and make it available for others.

Microbes themselves can also be food for bigger creatures. The role of microbes is a tricky part of keeping an aquarium. Water can have too many microbes. When this happens, water might look like a mess of green algae (AL-jee). Or, water can have too few microbes. That is bad for the creatures that rely on microbes. Keeping the right balance of microbes is hard.

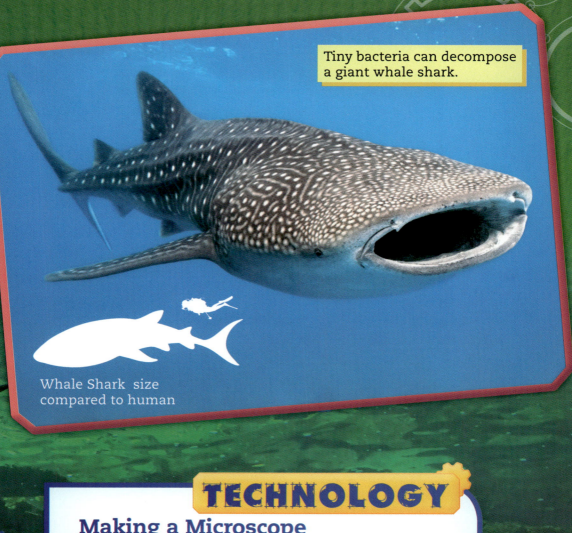

Tiny bacteria can decompose a giant whale shark.

Whale Shark size compared to human

TECHNOLOGY

Making a Microscope

Microbes were first discovered in the 1600s by Dutch scientist Anton van Leeuwenhoek (VAHN LEY-vuhn-hook). As a teenager working for a cloth merchant, he saw a simple microscope. It was a basic magnifying glass on a small stand. He learned to make his own microscopes. Soon, he discovered how to make very small glass spheres to use as lenses. These provided very strong magnification. He used his simple but powerful microscope to look at drops of water, where he discovered single-celled microbes.

Leeuwenhoek's microscope

Putting It All Together

There are many things to consider when putting an aquarium together. These include lighting, food, filters, temperature, and water movement.

Lights and Action!

The sun provides light and heat for Earth. Plants use light energy to make their own food. This process is called photosynthesis. Aquatic organisms, such as algae, use photosynthesis too. They have to live in parts of the oceans that get sunlight. Deeper in the water, light becomes dimmer. And even deeper, there is no sunlight at all. Creatures live in these depths, but there are fewer of them.

In tanks, people have to create artificial sunlight. It's a complicated job. There are different types of sunlight that organisms need to use as energy.

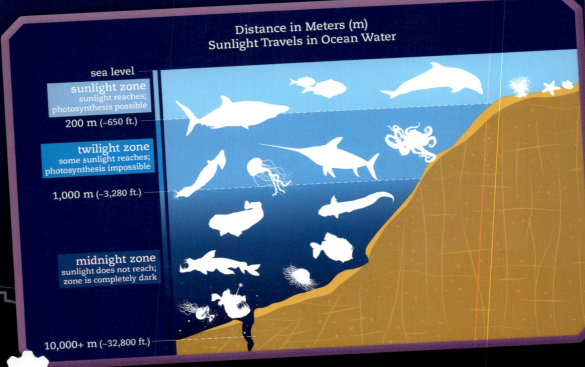

jellyfish in an aquarium tank

These types of light come from the visible spectrum—part of the **electromagnetic spectrum**. Different organisms need different parts of the spectrum for photosynthesis. For instance, green algae need mostly red light. But red algae use blue light. So, the lighting in tanks needs to cover most of the visible spectrum. Aquarists need to check light levels often to keep microbes happy and healthy.

SCIENCE

All the Colors of the Spectrum

Each color in the visible spectrum has a different **wavelength**. Red has the longest wavelength. Violet has the shortest. Water easily absorbs red light, so it does not travel very deep. But blue light reaches farther into the ocean. For this reason, a snorkeler's view under water looks much like the view above water. But scuba divers see a world of blue and black.

15

Aquarium lights also have to be strong. Electric lights are not nearly as bright as the sun. This means they have to work harder. In some aquariums, lights are on for as many as 15 hours each day. Aquariums that model coral reef ecosystems need the brightest tank lights. Those showing deep-water ecosystems need much less light.

Feeding Time

Many living creatures move to a new place if their current home doesn't have enough food. But moving is not a choice for creatures in tanks. And moving is not a choice for marine creatures such as coral, which cannot move at all. This can make feeding tank creatures a difficult task.

Ideally, a marine ecosystem exhibit would show an underwater world as it really exists. But most visitors want to see a lot of big, colorful animals. This means tanks have more creatures in small spaces than those habitats could normally support on their own. There are more fish, and the fish are bigger. There may be a lot of coral too. Many species have to compete for food. To prevent food shortages, aquarists regularly add food to tanks. This way, animals won't eat each other and visitors get to see a lot of sea creatures.

An aquarist feeds fish at Bueng Chawak Aquarium in Thailand.

Aquarists feed animals at the Melbourne Aquarium.

Many aquarium coral reefs are modeled after the Great Barrier Reef—the largest coral reef in the world. It is more than 2,000 kilometers (1,250 miles) long.

Adding extra food to tanks is known as **supplemental** feeding. The food might be frozen, freeze-dried, or even still alive. Fish will often get the most food. They are usually fed twice a day. Many types of coral feed on plankton. Plankton are organisms of any size that drift in a body of water and cannot swim against **tides**. But aquarium tanks are small and packed with animals that eat plankton. That can make it hard to keep enough plankton around for animals to eat.

The extra food added depends on the type of habitat in the exhibit. A coral reef exhibit may get a lot of extra baby shrimp every day. A seagrass ecosystem may need grass shrimp so slower animals, such as seahorses, get their share of food too.

Feeding schedules are an important part of keeping animals fed. They keep track of what type, how much, and when food is added to exhibits.

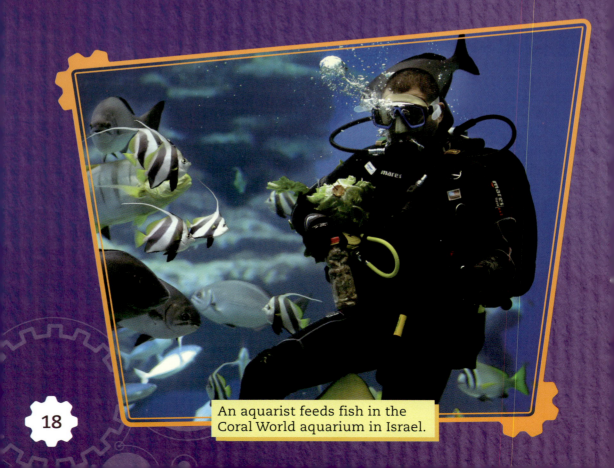

An aquarist feeds fish in the Coral World aquarium in Israel.

Having a Filter

Aquarists have another obstacle to overcome in tanks' enclosed spaces—a lot of waste products. This is why tank water must be filtered. The nitrogen cycle helps remove waste from water. Marine microbes, such as bacteria, change nitrogen into a form of the gas that phytoplankton use. Then, bigger creatures eat the phytoplankton, and the nitrogen moves through their bodies. But the nitrogen cycle can't remove all the waste products. That is where filters come in to help.

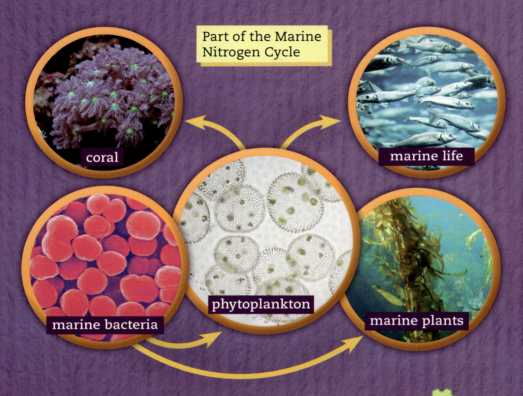

MATHEMATICS

How Many Fish Will Fit?

The general rule for home aquariums is that they should have no more than 5 cm of fish for every 7.4 liters of water, or 1 inch per gallon. But volume isn't the only thing to consider. The surface area of a tank is also important. A tall, thin tank has less surface area, which means more pollution from waste. A longer tank has more surface area.

Tank filters help remove aquatic animals' waste. Without filters, chemicals from animal waste can quickly reach **toxic** levels in tanks. High levels can cause algae blooms. Algae blooms happen when a lot of algae grow very quickly. They can disrupt entire ecosystems.

To prevent waste issues, water must be filtered. Many aquariums use turf algae—a type of microbe. They act as a biological filter. First, water from a tank moves along trays of turf algae outside the tank. Bright lights help the algae grow quickly. Then, the algae capture the extra nutrients, such as nitrogen. This helps to clean the water. Aquarists then harvest the algae. This removes any extra nitrogen. Finally, clean water is pumped back into the tank.

Algae filters also serve another important role. They produce oxygen and remove CO_2 from the water. This is important because fish need oxygen to breathe. And too much CO_2 can harm marine life.

Sometimes, aquariums use chemical filters instead of microbial filters. These filters often use charcoal. The charcoal captures waste and toxins from microbes. But chemical filters can remove useful nutrients too.

Since parrotfish eat coral, their waste is sand.

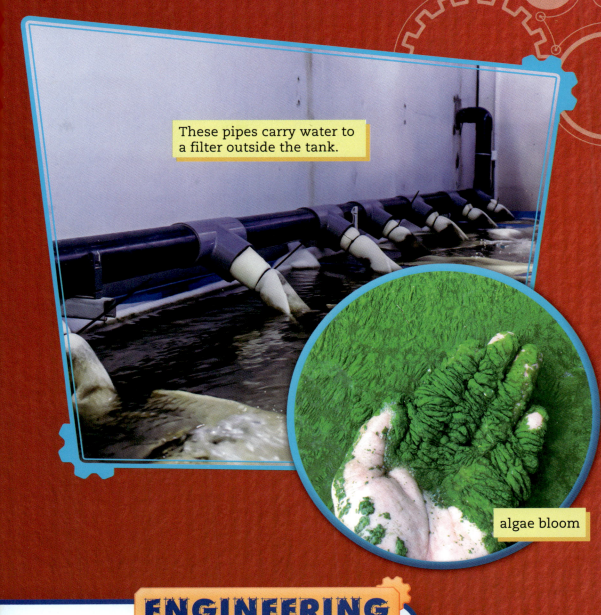

These pipes carry water to a filter outside the tank.

algae bloom

ENGINEERING
Adapting Turf Filters

Turf filters were created over 20 years ago by a scientist named Dr. Walter Adey and his team. However, they take a lot of space and can be noisy. People who have aquariums at home found them hard to use. So, engineers made changes to the design. They created a screen that hung vertically, with a waterfall-style pump. Today, these filters are engineered for home aquariums to be used in smaller spaces.

Temperatures and Tides

Water temperature is another important part of tank upkeep. Tank water needs to be the same temperature as the water where creatures live naturally. If water gets too warm or too cold, animals will die.

Sometimes, tanks have heaters to warm the water. Other times, aquarists have to chill water to keep it from getting too hot. It is not always that simple, though. For instance, coral reefs need cool water and bright light to grow. Overhead lights can be installed for coral reefs. But these lights give off a lot of heat. So, the water must be chilled to keep it from getting too hot.

A mudskipper swims in warm water.

A seal hugs a beluga whale in cold water.

Other habitats require cold water. Some river basins and streams are very cold. So, tanks need water chillers to create these low temperatures. It's a tricky balance.

Aquarists also have to consider water movement. In nature, tides, **currents**, and waves move water. Ocean water is constantly moving. The movement brings in fresh supplies of food and oxygen. It carries away dead matter and excess nutrients. In aquariums, pumps and filters keep water moving. They can also **simulate** waves and tidal cycles.

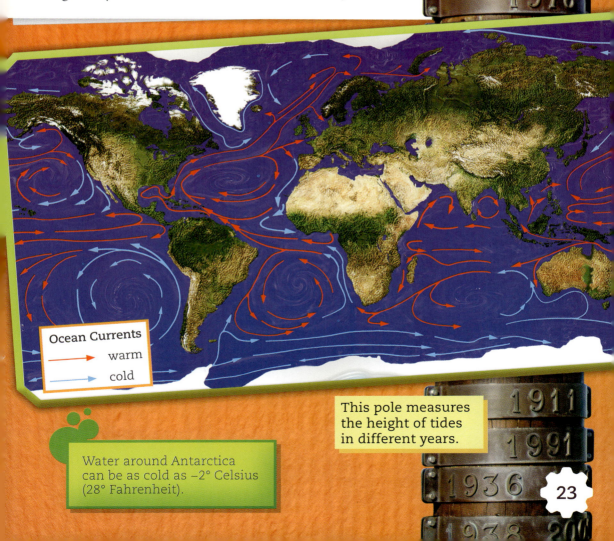

Ocean Currents
→ warm
→ cold

This pole measures the height of tides in different years.

Water around Antarctica can be as cold as −2° Celsius (28° Fahrenheit).

23

Changing Water

Ocean water contains salt. *Salinity* is the word that describes the amount of salt in water. The salinity of ocean water stays about the same all the time. But the salinity of places such as **estuaries** might change. It depends on tides and other factors. It's important that tanks have the correct salinity. Many factors can change the salinity of water in a tank. To make up for this, most aquarists need to add water and check salt levels frequently.

Once salinity is under control, aquarists have to make sure water in a tank stays clean. Filters and microbes help keep water clean, but aquarists still have to replace the water. Some aquarists replace about one-fifth of their tank water each year. To do so, some of it needs to be pumped out. Then, new water is filtered before it is pumped in. This helps add more nutrients. It makes up for those that marine creatures have used up. And it helps remove loose algae.

After aquarists have checked the salinity and cleanliness of a tank's water, they have to keep watch. They monitor these and other properties of water. Aquatic creatures depend on working equipment. Aquarists can help make sure that happens.

An aquarist checks the water at Waikiki Aquarium in Hawai'i.

This test shows the level of acidity in water.

Workers at Aquarium of the Pacific in California can test water from this private area.

An aquarist measures coral growth.

Most of the salt in ocean water comes from land. Rainwater carries salt particles from rocks into rivers, which flow into the sea.

25

Creatures Big and Small

Underwater worlds are mysterious and hidden. There is so much life in the oceans' depths. The biggest creatures in the world live in oceans. Mammoth blue whales dwell in its waters. The smallest creatures live in oceans too. The underwater world needs these mighty marine microbes.

Aquariums help people understand this world. They give people a close-up of coral reefs. They show people bright jellyfish. They help people learn about marine ecosystems and how they change. Aquariums show people how humans affect life under water. They teach people that what they do on land affects what happens in oceans.

At aquariums, colorful fish draw people into this world. Jellies and seahorses are interesting to watch. But look deeper. Are algae filtering the water? Are pumps creating currents like those in the ocean? What smaller creatures are part of this world? Even when you look as close as you can, remember: there are tiny microbes too small for your eyes to see. There is so much more hidden in this world. What can we do to make sure it stays healthy?

Aquarium visitors watch a sunfish swim.

Scuba divers explore ocean life near Monterey Bay Aquarium in California.

marine microbes under a microscope

Humans have explored only one-twentieth of the ocean biome!

27

STEAM CHALLENGE

Define the Problem

Imagine you are an aquarist at the Georgia Aquarium, the largest aquarium in the United States. Your task is to maintain the coral reef exhibit. The fish are fed a meal of frozen brine shrimp twice daily. The frozen shrimp are stored far from the exhibit, and you are looking for an effective way to transport the frozen shrimp.

Constraints: The interior of your container must be at least 20 centimeters (8 inches) across to maximize the amount of shrimp you can carry in one trip.

Criteria: A successful container will prevent ice from melting for 15 minutes.

Research and Brainstorm

How do aquarists make sure that all organisms in an exhibit are fed? Is it important for a container to be closed during transport? How will you carry the container?

Design and Build

Sketch your container design. What purpose will each part serve? What materials will work best? Build the model.

Test and Improve

Place an ice cube in the container and allow it to remain undisturbed for 15 minutes. Then, measure any water in the container. Did it work? How can you improve it? Modify your design and try again.

Reflect and Share

Which parts of your model worked best to slow the melting of the ice cube? Could your model be used to prevent ice from melting for a longer period of time? What do you think would happen if you added multiple ice cubes to your model?

Glossary

acidic—an imbalance in water that contains potentially harmful chemicals and can affect plant life

atmosphere—the entire mass of air around Earth

biomass—the amount of living matter in a certain area

cannibals—animals that eat other animals of their own kind

currents—continuous movement of water in the same direction

decomposition—the process that causes something to slowly be destroyed and broken down into smaller parts

ecosystems—all the living and nonliving things in particular environments

electromagnetic spectrum—a way of grouping all energy and light waves

estuaries—areas where rivers meet seas

mangrove—a type of tropical tree that grows in coastal swamps and shallow seawater

marine—relating to the sea or the plants and animals that live in the sea

molecules—the smallest possible amounts of things that still have all the things' characteristics

simulate—to look, feel, or behave like something else

supplemental—acting to complete something

tides—the regular upward and downward movements of the level of the oceans

toxic—poisonous

wavelength—the distance between energy or light waves

Index

Adey, Dr. Walter, 21

algae, 12, 14–15, 20–21, 24, 26

Antarctica, 23

Aquarium of the Pacific, 25

bacteria, 5, 10–13, 19

Bueng Chawak Aquarium, 17

California, 25, 27

carbon cycle, 8

carbon dioxide (CO_2), 8–9, 12, 20

chemical filters, 20

Coral World, 18

decomposition, 12

electromagnetic spectrum, 15

Great Barrier Reef, 17

Hawai'i, 24

Israel, 18

lighting, 14–16, 20, 22

marine microbial ecology, 10

Melbourne Aquarium, 17

Monterey Bay Aquarium, 27

nitrogen cycle, 10–12, 19

photosynthesis, 14–15

supplemental feeding, 18

temperature, 14, 22–23

Thailand, 17

turf filters, 21

van Leeuwenhoek, Anton, 13

Waikiki Aquarium, 24

waste, 19–20

31

CAREER ADVICE
from Smithsonian

Do you want to help aquatic animals?
Here are some tips to get you started.

"In school, I loved learning about animals and how healthy ecosystems worked. I earned my degrees in marine biology—studying the animals of oceans and estuaries. To understand ecosystems, you need to learn biology, chemistry, geology, botany, behavior, and math."
—*Jessica Lunt, Marine Biologist*

"Try to visit museums, zoos, and aquariums wherever you go. The experiences might show you that there are interesting animals or places you hadn't thought about. Microbes can seem small and boring at first, but they can be beautiful and are important indicators of an ecosystem's health." —*Carol Baldwin, Research Zoologist*